Methodist Episcopal Church

Minutes of the Sixteenth Session of the Holston Conference

of the Methodist Episcopal Church

Methodist Episcopal Church

Minutes of the Sixteenth Session of the Holston Conference
of the Methodist Episcopal Church

ISBN/EAN: 9783337848798

Printed in Europe, USA, Canada, Australia, Japan

Cover: Foto ©Lupo / pixelio.de

More available books at **www.hansebooks.com**

MINUTES

OF THE

SIXTEENTH ANNUAL SESSION

OF THE

HOLSTON CONFERENCE

OF THE

METHODIST EPISCOPAL CHURCH,

HELD AT

GREENEVILLE, TENN., OCT. 20-24, 1880.

KNOXVILLE, TENN.:

WHIG AND CHRONICLE STEAM BOOK AND JOB PRINTING OFFICE.

1880.

Officers of the Conference.

Bishop E. O. HAVEN. D.D. L.L.D.. President.

JAS. D. ROBERSON, Secretary.

E. M. LOCKWOOD, Assistant Secretary.

J. S. HILL,   ⎫
               ⎬ Statistical Secretaries.
W. T. SENTER. ⎭

Officers of Conference Societies.

MISSIONARY SOCIETY.

J. W. MANN.	PRESIDENT.
J. B. LITTLE.	VICE PRESIDENT.
J. S. PETTY,	SECRETARY.
S. TINKER.	TREASURER.

BOARD OF CHURCH EXTENSION.

J. W. RAMSEY, *Cleveland*,	PRESIDENT.
S. TINKER.	VICE PRESIDENT.
E. M. |LOCKWOOD.	SECRETARY.
J. J. MANKER.	TREASURER.

J. H. HORNSBY, *Athens*.
P. C. WILSON, *Chattanooga*.
WM. RULE, *Knoxville*.
G. W. HENNINGER, and the PRESIDING ELDERS, *ex-officio*.

TO PREACH THE MISSIONARY SERMON.

J. W. MANN.   ALTERNATE. J. A. RUBLE.

EDUCATION SOCIETY.

JOHN F. SPENCE,	PRESIDENT.
T. S. WALKER,	VICE PRESIDENT.
J. W. MANN.	SECRETARY.
J. S. PETTY.	TREASURER.

SABBATH SCHOOL SOCIETY.

J. B. FORD.	PRESIDENT.
T. S. WALKER.	VICE PRESIDENT.
J. C. WRIGHT.	SECRETARY.
B. CRIST.	TREASURE R

TRUSTEES OF CONFERENCE.

EXAMINING COMMITTEES FOR 1881.

For Admission on Trial.—J. F. SPENCE, M. A. RULE, E. B. CLARK.

First Year.—T. H. RUSSELL. J. C. WRIGHT, J. F. PERRY.

Second Year.—C. B. SPARROW, J. M. DURHAM. H. H. BURK.

Third Year.—E. M. LOCKWOOD. B. CRIST, T. R. WEST.

Fourth Year.—P. H. REED. J. R. HUGHES, M. SEATON.

Local Deacons.—T. H. HODGE. JAS. D. ROBERSON. J. D. LAWSON.

Local Elders.—T. W. BROWN. J. H. JENNINGS. D. S. HODESDEN.

TRIERS OF APPEALS.

J. A. RUBLE,   W. C. GRAVES,   J. J. MANKER, N. G. TAYLOR,   T. S. WALKER.

ORDER OF TAKING COLLECTIONS.

First Quarter.—Sunday School and Tract.

Second Quarter.—Episcopal Fund and Freedmen's Aid Society.

Third Quarter.—Missionary and Church Extension.

Fourth Quarter.—Education and Conference Claimants.

Collection to Pay off the judgment against the Trustees at Johnson City to be taken during January.

CONFERENCE ROLL.

1. Robert O. Ayers, Chatata, Tenn.
2. Jonathan N. Baker, Chucky Valley, Tenn.
3. William B. Ballenger, Cleveland, Tenn.
4. Lem. Bogart, Sevierville, Tenn.
5. Thomas W. Brown, Parrottsville, Tenn.
6. Andrew J. Bruner, Laurel Gap, Tenn.
7. Hilton H. Burk, Loudon, Tenn.
8. Milton R. M. Burk, Half Moon Island, Roane county, Tenn.
9. J. W. Burnett, Pikeville, Tenn.
10. L. B. Caldwell, Athens, Tenn.
11. J. L. Cardwell, Home, Greene county, Tenn.
12. Dan'l Carter,† Flat Gap, Tenn.
13. Thos. A. Cass, Athens, Tenn.
14. Elbert B. Clark, Knoxville, Tenn.
15. G. W. Coleman,* Athens, Tenn.
16. Francis M. Cones, Thorn Town, Indiana.
17. B. Crist, Clinton, Tenn.
18. William C. Daily, Knoxville, Tenn.
19. James M. Durham, Knoxville, Tenn.
20. J. B. Fitzgerald, Fullen's, Tenn.
21. John B. Ford, Cleveland, Tenn.
22. John Forrester, Glades, Tenn.
23. W. C. Graves, Morristown, Tenn.
24. A. J. Greer, Tazewell, Tenn.
25. Samuel Greear, Robertsville, Anderson county, Tenn.
26. Robert H. Guthrie, Harrison, Tenn.
27. W. M. Haskell, Knoxville, Tenn.
28. George W. Heninger, Russellville, Tenn.
29. S. Henry, Maryville, Tenn.
30. P. H. Henry, Maryville, Tenn.
31. T. H. Hodge, Cleveland, Tenn.
32. David S. Hodsden, Sevierville, Tenn.
33. J. R. Hughes, Rheatown, Tenn.
34. Samuel W. Hyden, Maryville, Tenn.
35. G. W. Jarvis, Speedwell, Tenn.
36. John H. Jennings, New Market, Tenn.
37. George Julian, Cleveland, Tenn.
38. Wm. Kinsland, Spring House, Tenn.
39. James D. Lawson, Wear's Valley, Tenn.
40. J. B. Little, Fincastle, Tenn.
41. Edwin M. Lockwood, Cleveland, Tenn.
42. Wm. R. Long, Ducktown, Tenn.
43. Wm. Lucas, Delaware, Ohio.
44. J. W. Mann, Jonesboro', Tenn.
45. John J. Manker, Chattanooga, Tenn.
46. Joseph P. Milburn, Graysburg, Tenn.
47. J. N. Moore, Knoxville, Tenn.
48. John F. Morrison, Locust Spring, Tenn.
49. Joseph A. Nicholson, Victoria, Tenn.
50. James F. Perry, Washington, Tenn.
51. Adam C. Peters, Glades, Morgan county, Tenn.
52. John S. Petty, Greeneville, Tenn.

53. R. Pierce, New Market, Tenn.
54. *Henry Pyle*, Loy's X Roads, Tenn.
55. Patrick H. Reed, Flat Gap, Tenn.
56. Daniel Richardson.
57. James D. Roberson, Jonesboro', Tenn.
58. Jas. J. Robinett, Kingston, Tenn.
59. J. A. Ruble, Knoxville, Tenn.
60. Matthew A. Rule, Rogersville, Tenn.
61. Thomas H. Russell, Knoxville, Tenn.
62. Thomas B. Russell, Greeneville, Tenn.
63. S. B. Scott, Jamestown, Tenn.
64. James B. Seaton, Ellijoy, Tenn.
65. M. Seaton, Horse Creek, Tenn.
66. W. T. Senter, Panther Springs, Tenn.
67. *Wm. D. Smith*, Cleveland, Tenn.
68. C. B. Sparrow, Knoxville, Tenn.
69. J. F. Spence, Knoxville, Tenn.
70. W. Stark, Crossville, Tenn.
71. G. M. Stone, Pin Hook, Tenn.
72. Thomas S. Walker, Knoxville, Tenn.
73. Albert G. Watkins, Mossy Creek, Tenn.
74. BENJAMIN F. WELLS, Asheville, North Carolina.
75. T. R. West, Tampico, Tenn.
76. Rufus M. Witt, Coco Creek, Tenn.
77. *Absalom B. Wright*, Travisville, Tenn.
78. J. C. Wright, Rheatown, Tenn.

PROBATIONERS.

J. A. Baker, Harrison, Tenn.
J. S. Hill, Elizabethton, Tenn.
Lucius H. Massey, New Market, Tenn.

C. D. Munsey, Taylorsville, Tenn.
I. C. Patton, Telford, Tenn.
R. C. Robertson.

---

* Names in *Italics* are Supernumeraries.
† Names in SMALL CAPITALS are Superannuates.

APPOINTMENTS.

Chattanooga District.

R. Pierce, Presiding Elder, P. O., New Market, Tenn.

Athens, Sydney Tinker.

Athens Circuit and Riceville, to be supplied.

Blue Springs, R. O. Ayres.

Chatata, G. M. Stone, G. Julian, Supernumerary.

Chattanooga, J. J. Manker.

Cleveland, T. H. Hodge.

Cleveland Circuit, E. M. Lockwood, W. D. Smith, Supernumerary.

Ducktown, to be supplied.

Madisonville, J. N. Moore.

Ooltewah, J. A. Baker.

Sewee, W. R. Long.

J. F. Spence, President; L. B. Caldwell, Professor in East Tennessee Wesleyan University and members of Athens Quarterly Conference.

J. B. Ford, Agent of the Sunday School Union; member of the Cleveland Quarterly Conference.

M. R. M. Burk, Principal of Johnson Seminary; member of Blue Spring Quarterly Conference.

Greeneville District.

J. W. Mann, Presiding Elder, P. O., Greeneville, Tenn.

Elizabethton, J. S. Hill.

Fall Branch, M. Seaton.

Greeneville, J. S. Petty.

Greeneville Circuit, T. B. Russell.

Irvin, to be supplied.

Johnson City Circuit, J. L. Cardwell.

Jonesboro Circuit, J. C. Patton, J. N. Baker.

Kingsport, J. P. Milburn.

Parrottsville, T. W. Brown.

Rheatown, J. R. Hughes, J. B. Fitzgerald.

St. Clair, A. J. Bruner.

Taylorsville, C. D. Munsey.

J. C. Wright, Principal of Rheatown Seminary, and member of Rheatown Quarterly Conference.

Kingston District.

W. C. Daily, Presiding Elder, P. O., Knoxville, Tenn.

Battle Creek, W. B. Ballenger.

Crossville, W. Stark.

Dayton, J. A. Nicholson.

Hamilton, D. Richardson.

Jamestown, S. B. Scott, A. B. Wright, Supernumerary.

Jasper, J. F. Perry.

Kingston, J. J. Robinett.

Kingston Circuit, T. H. Russell.

Pikeville, J. W. Burnett.

Rugby and Huntsville, to be supplied.

Scarborough, S. Greear.

Wartburg, to be supplied, A. C. Peters, Supernumerary.

Knoxville District.

J. A. Ruble, Presiding Elder, P. O., Knoxville, Tenn.

Campbell Station, R. C. Robertson.

Fair Garden, J. D. Lawson.

Knox Circuit, A. G. Watkins.

Knoxville, 1st Church, C. B. Sparrow.
Knoxville. 2d Church, J. M. Durham.
London, H. H. Burk.
Little River, E. B. Clark.
Maryville, P. H. Henry.
New Market, J. H. Jennings.
Newport. J. B. Seaton.
Sevierville, D. S. Hodsden. .
Thorn Grove, P. H. Reed.
L. H. Massey, Professor in Holston
   Seminary: member of New Mar-
   ket Quarterly Conference.

POWELL'S VALLEY DISTRICT.

T. S. WALKER, Presiding Elder,
  P. O.. Well Spring, Tenn.
Big Valley, A. J. Greer,
Clinton. B. Crist.

Fincastle and Spe'dwell, G. W. Jarvis.
Jacksboro', T. A. Cass.
Maynardville, W. Kinsland.
Morristown, G. W. Heninger.
Rogersville Circuit, M. A. Rule.*
Rutledge. W. T. Senter.
Sneedville, J. H. Amis.
Tazewell. T. R. West.
Thorn Hill, L. Bogart.

C. S. Long, Missionary to Japan.
R. J. Cooke, transferred to the Geor-
  gia Conference.
J. R. Shultz, transferred to the Kan-
  sas Conference.
N. G. Taylor, transferred to the Blue
  Ridge Conference.
M. W. Broyles, transferred to the
  Blue Ridge Conference.

DISCIPLINARY QUESTIONS.

1. *Who are received by transfer, and from what Conference?*
Sydney Tinker, from the South East Indiana Conference.

2. *Who are admitted on trial?*
Lucius H. Massey.

3. *Who remain on trial?*
J. S. Hill, C. D. Munsey, R. C. Robertson. J. A. Baker, and I. C. Patton.

4. *Who are discontinued?*
Burr Williams.

5. *Who are admitted into full connection?*
J. J. Robinett, Pleasant H. Henry, J. A. Nicholson and J. W. Burnett.

6. *Who are re-admitted?*
I. C. Patton.

7. *Who are received on credentials from other Churches?*
None.

8. *What traveling preachers have been elected Deacons?*
John W. Burnett and J. J. Robinett.

9. *What traveling preachers have been ordained Deacons?*
The two elected.

10. *What local preachers have been elected Deacons?*
Joshua Linebaugh and Joseph W. Fraker.

11. *What local preachers have been ordained Deacons?*
The two elected.

12. *Who are the traveling Deacons of the first class?*
S. B. Scott. Geo. M. Stone. J. J. Robinett, J. W. Burnett and J. A. Nicholson.

13. *Who are the traveling Deacons of the second class?*
Geo. W. Jarvis. W. T. Senter, and Mark W. Broyles.

14. *What traveling Deacons have been elected Elders?*
Albert G. Watkins and Wilson Stark.

15. *What traveling Deacons have been ordained Elders?*
The two elected.

16. *What local Deacons have been elected Elders?*
Arnold P. Little and Charles E. Johnson.

17. *What local Deacons have been ordained Elders?*
The two elected.

18. *Who are the supernumerary preachers?*
F. M. Cones, W. Lucas, J. F. Morrison, W. D. Smith, A. B. Wright and Henry Pyle.

19. *Who are the superannuated preachers?*
Daniel Carter, Robert H. Guthrie, Spencer Henry and Benjamin F. Wells.

20. *Was the character of each preacher examined?*
This was strictly done, as the name of each preacher was called in open Conference.

21. *Have any died?*
None.

22. *Have any been transferred, and to what Conferences?*
R. J. Cook to Georgia Conference; J. R. Shultz to Kansas Conference; N. G. Taylor and M. W. Broyles to Blue Ridge Conference.

23. *Have any withdrawn?*
None.

24. *Have any located at their own request?*
Geo. W. Coleman.

25. *Have any been located?*
None.

26. *Have any been permitted to withdraw under charges?*
None.

27. *Have any been expelled?*
None.

28. *Who are the Triers of Appeals?*
J. A. Ruble, W. C. Graves, J. J. Manker, W. C. Daily, J. W. Mann, N. G. Taylor, and T. S. Walker.

29. *What is the Statistical Report?*
[See tabulated statement.]

30. *What are the claims on the Conference fund?*

31. *What has been reecived on these claims, and how has it been applied?*
$158 95 received, which has been applied under order of the Conference.

32. *Where are the preachers stationed?*
[See appointments.]

33. *Where shall the next Conference be held?*
Maryville, Tennessee.

DAILY PROCEEDINGS.

FIRST DAY.

M. E. CHURCH, GREENEVILLE, TENNESSEE,
WEDNESDAY, October 20, 1880.

The Holston Annual Conference of the Methodist Episcopal Church convened in its sixteenth session this morning at 9 o'clock.

The presiding Bishop, E. O. Haven, D. D., read, in opening the Conference, the fifth chapter of First Peter, and announced the 574th hymn, after the singing of which Bishop H. W. Warren, D. D., led in prayer.

The Conference then joined in singing the 726th hymn, and Bishop Haven offered prayer.

The Secretary of last session called the roll, and seventy-six members and probationers responded to their names.

J. J. Manker and J. W. Mann having been nominated for the secretaryship, and both having respectfully declined to accept the office, Jas. D. Roberson was elected Secretary, and E. M. Lockwood, Assistant Secretary.

The bar of the Conference was fixed to extend to the front side of the third pair of windows.

Conference decided to meet for its daily sessions at 8:30 A. M., and adjourn at 12 M.

The usual committees were appointed as follows:

EDUCATION—C. B. Sparrow, J. F. Spence, B. Crist, J. J. Manker, E. M. Lockwood, L. B. Caldwell, R. Pierce, Prof. Joseph H. Ketron.

CHURCH EXTENSION—S. Tinker, Wm. Kinsland, D. Richardson.

FREEDMEN'S AID SOCIETY—J. H. Jennings, G. W. Heninger, D. B. Lawton.

TEMPERANCE—W. Bluford, D. S. Hodsden, J. F. Spence.

MISSIONS—The Presiding Elders.

SUNDAY SCHOOLS—A. J. Greer, T. H. Hodge, J. B. Ford.

TRACTS—J. S. Hill, J. J. Robinett, G. W. Jarvis.
BOOK CONCERN ACCOUNTS.—J. B. Little, D. S. Hodsden.
AUDITING.—S. Greear, M. A. Rule, M. Williams.
STEWARDS—W. M. Haskell, Lemuel Bogart, A. J. Fletcher.
POST OFFICES—A. G. Watkins, J. B. Seaton, J. N. Baker, J. A. Nicholson, B. H. Johnson, Henry Jones.
PUBLIC WORSHIP—J. W. Mann, J. J. Manker, J. A. Ruble, C. K. Mays.
CHURCH LITERATURE—Ralph Pierce, J. B. Ford, E. M. Lockwood.
AMERICAN BIBLE SOCIETY—P. H. Henry, J. R. Hughes, W. H. Rodgers, J. J. Manker, J. S. Hill, A. J. Bruner.
NEW YORK BOOK CONCERN ACCOUNT—J. D. Lawson.
EPISCOPAL FUND—J. M. Durham.
DISTRICT CONFERENCE RECORDS—J. F. Spence, J. S. Petty, W. M. Haskell.

Rev. Dr. Geo. S. Savage, Agent of the American Bible Society, was introduced to the Conference, and gave a very interesting and instructive account of the work of the Society in Tennessee and Kentucky. He stated that the Holston Conference of the M. E. Church took proportionably the largest number of collections for the Society of any of the six white Conferences within the bounds of the territory under his superintendence.

J. A. Ruble read a paper concerning the Fountain Head Church property, on the Knox Circuit, upon which was raised the following committee: J. A. Ruble, J. W. Mann, J. J. Manker, T. S. Walker.

The Twentieth Question was taken up, and J. S. Petty, after the passage of his character, gave an interesting account of the work on the Chattanooga District.

The characters of W. R. Long, R. O. Ayres, E. M. Lockwood and Geo. Julian were passed.

The names of T. W. Brown, F. R. West and P. H. Reed were called and their characters passed.

After the passage of his character J. A. Ruble gave an encouraging report of the Knoxville District.

The characters of C. B. Sparrow, J. M. Durham, J. B. Little, J. B. Seaton, W. C. Graves, E. B. Clark, D. S. Hodsden, J. H. Jennings, J. D. Lawson, J. N. Moore and T. H. Hodge were severally passed.

The character of T. S. Walker was passed, and he gave a favorable report of the Powell's Valley District.

On motion. a committee of three on Conference Relations was ordered.

G. W. Coleman, at his own request, was granted a certificate of location.

Question Eighteenth was taken up, and W. B. Ballenger was made effective.

F. M. Comes. W. Lucas, J. F. Morrison, W. D. Smith and A. B. Wright were continued in the supernumerary relation.

After various announcements, Conference adjourned, Dr. G. S. Savage pronouncing the benediction.

SECOND DAY.

THURSDAY, October 21, 1880.

Conference met at 8:30 A. M.   The devotional service was conducted by W. C. Daily.

The minutes of the previous session were read and approved.

The roll of absentees was called. and eight additional members were found present.

On motion. the further calling of the roll was discontinued.

J. M. Freeman, D. D., Assistant Secretary of the Sunday School Union of the Methodist Episcopal Church, was introduced to the Conference.

R. Pierce and L. B. Caldwell were added to the Committee on Freedmen's Aid Society.

The Secretary read a paper from the Corresponding Secretary of the Freedmen's Aid Society, and one from the Treasurers of the Episcopal Fund. which were referred to their appropriate committees.

The Assistant Secretary read the annual report of the Book Concern. and it was referred to the Committee on Church Literature.

A petition from the chairman of the National Temperance Association was read and referred to the Committee on Temperance.

S. Tinker was made Treasurer of the Missionary Society.

Conference resumed the consideration of the Twentieth Question.

J. W. Mann, after the approval of his character, read a report of the Greeneville District.

J. J. Manker, T. B. Russell, J. B. Fitzgerald, M. Seaton, A. J. Bruner, Jas. D. Roberson, G. W. Heninger, J. R. Hughes, J. P. Milburn, J. N. Baker and J. L. Cardwell were called and their characters passed.

The character of Thomas H. Russell was passed, and he represented the Kingston District as being in a prosperous condition.

The characters of S. Greear, A. C. Peters, D. Richardson, T. A. Cass, J. C. Tate and J. F. Perry were severally passed.

The name of H. H. Burk having been called, on motion a Committee of Enquiry was asked for in his case.

On motion, the Committee on Conference Relations was increased to six, and the Bishop announced the following as said committee: E. M. Lockwood, O. N. Hypsher, J. J. Manker, J. H. Jennings, Wm. Kinsland and J. F. Perry.

The case of W. R. Long was referred to the Committee on Conference Relations.

The case of S. J. Harris was referred to the Presiding Elders.

Rev. A. J. Nugent, of the United Brethren, was introduced to the Conference.

After the passage of his character, C. K. Mays read a good report of the Russellville District.

The character of Wm. Bluford was passed.

On motion, the Conference devoted some time in taking up the Statistical Reports.

Question Third was taken up and J. M. Baker, Charles Boyd, Handy N. Brown, Anthony Douglas, Alex. Gillespie, J. S. Hill, Henry Jones, C. D. Munsey, R. C. Robertson, Miles Williams and J. W. Wells were continued on trial.

Burr Williams was discontinued.

Under Question Fifth Pleasant H. Henry and J. J. Robinett were recommended for full membership and elected to Deacon's Orders.

J. A. Nicholson having been ordained Local Deacon, was recommended for full membership.

Under Fourteenth Question A. G. Watkins was elected to Elder's Orders.

On motion, the Triars of Appeals of the past year were all continued for the ensuing year, except F. M. Fanning, whose place was supplied by T. S. Walker.

A. C. Peters was granted a supernumerary relation.

J. B. Little was granted leave of absence.

On motion, a Committee on Memoirs of the late deceased wives of the members of the Conference was ordered, and W. C. Daily, J. B. Ford and J. W. Mann were appointed.

After the usual announcements, the Conference adjourned, with the benediction by S. Tinker.

THIRD DAY.

Friday, October 22, 1880.

Conference met at the usual hour. N. G. Taylor, D. D., conducted the devotional exercises.

The minutes of the previous session were read and approved.

The committee in the case of H. H. Burk were announced by the Bishop as follows: D. Richardson, S. Greear and J. F. Perry.

The Bishop stated that the Conference was authorized to draw on the Chartered Fund for $30, and a draft for that amount was ordered.

The Twentieth Question was resumed and the character of W. C. Daily was passed.

Question Fifteenth was resumed and Wilson Stark was elected to Elder's Orders.

S. J. Harris read a good and interesting account of his labors during the past year, and of the condition of the Cleveland District.

Question Fifth was resumed and J. W. Burnett was recommended for full membership and elected for Deacon's Orders.

The Thirteenth Question was taken up and J. Fletcher. O. N. Hypsher, Geo. W. Jarvis, Alex. Jordan. Wm. T. Senter and Mark W. Broyles were advanced to the Deacons of second class.

Jacob Mann was located at his own request.

S. B. Scott and Geo. M. Stone were continued Deacons of the first class.

The case of Clemm Shaw was referred to the Committee on Conference Relations.

The committee in the case of H. H. Burk presented their report. and after its adoption the character of Brother Burk was passed.

J. A. Ruble read the report of the committee on the Fountain Head Church property, and it was adopted.

The members of the class to be ordained Deacons were called forward, and after an earnest and excellent address to them by Bishop Haven he propounded to them the disciplinary questions for ordination to Deacon's Orders.

Rev. J. M. Freeman, D. D., delivered an able and timely address to the Conference on the Sunday School and Tract interests.

The Second Question was taken up and Lucius H. Massey. William T. Marley, Ben. H. Johnson and Jacob Pate, having been properly recommended by their respective District Conferences and favorably represented by the Examining Committee and their Presiding Elders. were admitted on trial.

I. C. Patton was re-admitted on trial and placed in the class of the second year.

A. J. Greer and J. B. Fitzgerald were added to the Committee on Examination for Local Deacons' Orders.

The Statistical Secretary was authorized to use the minutes of last year where there were no reports.

After the usual announcements, Conference adjourned. Spencer Henry pronouncing the benediction.

FOURTH DAY.

SATURDAY. October 23. 1880.

Conference met at the appointed hour.   C. B. Sparrow conducted the devotional services.

The minutes of the preceding session were read and approved.

Rev. J. O. A. Clark, D. D., of the M. E. Church. South. Agent of the Savannah Memorial Church. was introduced to the Conference. and delivered an instructive address concerning the Wesley Memorial Volume.

Rev. Mr. Bulger, of the United Brethren. was introduced to the Conference.

Question Eleventh was taken up and Anthony Douglas. Joshua Linebaugh, Lawson Cobb. Benjamin H. Johnson. Handy N. Brown. Alexander Gillespie and Joseph W. Fraker. having been favorably represented by the Examining Committee and properly recommended by their District Conferences, were elected for Local Deacon's Orders.

Under the consideration of Question Sixteenth Arnold P. Little and Charles E. Johnson were elected for Local Elder's Orders.

On motion, the Conference entered upon the consideration of the division of the Conference.

J. J. Manker offered a resolution for the organization of an East Tennessee Annual Conference. which was unanimously adopted.

Joseph W. Wells was recommended for admission into full membership.

Jas. Yarnell was re-admitted on certificate of location.

Alex. Lindsey was admitted on credentials from the Zion Church.

William Mills was admitted on credentials from the Baptist Church. and placed in the class of the Deacons of the first year.

The committee in the case of S. J. Harris presented their report recommending the passage of his character, which was adopted.

On motion of J. F. Spence, a committee of five on church property was ordered, part of which to be selected from the Holston and part from the East Tennessee Conference.

The report of the Committee on Temperance was read by J. F. Spence, and the same approved.

The Bishop announced the following as the joint committee for the two Conferences on Church Property: W. H. Rodgers, J. J. Manker, S. J. Harris, J. F. Spence, C. K. Mays.

R. Pierce read the report of the Committee on the Episcopal Fund, and it was approved.

On motion of J. A. Ruble, the credentials of J. M. Hill was ordered to be restored to him.

The report of the Committee on Sunday Schools was read by J. B. Bord, and the same adopted.

B. F. Well's character was passed, and he was continued in the relation of a superannuated preacher.

L. B. Caldwell presented the report of the Committee on Education, and it was adopted.

On motion, C. B. Sparrow was authorized to sign the names of the members of the Conference to a petition to the Legislature of the State of Tennessee for the establishment of a Reformatory School for friendless youths.

The report of the Committee on Freedmen's Aid Society was read by G. W. Heninger, and it was approved.

Various announcements were made, and the Conference adjourned, with the benediction by Dr. J. O. A. Clark.

AFTERNOON SESSION.

Conference met at 2 P. M., N. G. Taylor, by appointment of the Bishop, presiding. B. Crist conducted the devotional service.

The minutes were read and approved.

Resolutions relating to Conference Claimants and the order of taking the collections were offered by C. B. Sparrow and adopted.

E. M. Lockwood read the report of the Committee on Tracts, which was adopted.

On motion, the Committee on Conference Claimants were

ordered to pay the burial expenses of Sister Fortner. deceased.

G. W. Heninger read the report of the Committee on Church Literature. and E. Q. Fuller, D. D., Editor of the *Methodist Advocate*, Atlanta, Georgia, was introduced to the Conference and spoke ably on the subject of the report, after which it was adopted.

J. J. Manker read the report of the Committee on Church Extension, which was adopted.

The report of the Committee on Conference Relations was read by Wm. Kinsland. which. after some discussion. was recommitted for further consideration.

Conference adjourned, to meet at 6:30 P. M.. J. F. Spence pronouncing the benediction.

EVENING SESSION.

Conference met at the appointed hour. and W. H. Haskell conducted the worship.

The minutes of the afternoon session were read and approved.

On motion of the Secretary. the roll was called and subscriptions for the publication of the minutes were taken.

The Bishop announced the names of the Board of Church Extension and the several examining committees for the ensuing year.

W. M. Haskell read the report of the Committee on Conference Claimants. which was adopted.

The money was distributed as follows:

Mrs. Dungan, $20, paid to J. W. Mann.
Mrs. Marshall, $18, paid to J. S. Petty.
Mrs. Milburn. $20, paid to J. L. Caldwell.
Mrs. Fair, $10, paid to A. J. Fletcher.
Mrs. Patterson, $10, paid to A. J. Fletcher.
Mrs. Murphey, $10, paid to J. A. Ruble.
Mrs. Cobleigh. $28, paid to L. B. Caldwell.
R. H. Guthrie. $12.75. paid to Book Concern.
Spencer Henry, $12, paid to himself.
B. F. Wells, $8. paid to T. F. Roberson.
D. B. Lawton, $10.20, paid to himself.

J. A. Ruble read a paper concerning the debt of the Trustees at Johnson City, which was adopted.

D. S. Hodsden read the report of the Committee on the American Bible Society, which, after an instructive address by W. H. Rodgers, was adopted.

The Committee on Conference Relations was discharged and the same committee was re-appointed, to report at the next annual session of the Conference.

Maryville was selected as the place for holding the next Conference.

Henry Pyle was granted a supernumerary relation.

On motion of R. Pierce, the Treasurer of the Conference Educational Society was instructed to pay to the Financial Agent of the Holston Seminary the cash collection of this year as per resolution of last Conference.

On motion, the money of the benevolent collections entered after the completion of the statistical report was ordered sent to the proper authorities and the amount embodied in the reports at the next Conference.

The statistical report was read and approved.

A number of resolutions of thanks were offered and adopted, various announcements were made, and the Conference adjourned to meet at 7 o'clock the following evening.

Bishop Haven pronounced the benediction.

FIFTH DAY.

MONDAY, October 25, 1880.

After preaching by J. M. Freeman, D. D., Sabbath evening, the Bishop called the Conference to order.

The minutes of the previous session were read and approved.

The Committee on Missions presented their report and the same, on motion, was adopted.

J. W. Mann read a memoir of Julia T. Manker, which was approved and ordered printed in the Minutes of the Conference.

The Committee on Memoirs expressed their regret at being unable to read at the present session the memoir of Sister J. H. Jennings, and were granted the privilege of having it published in the Conference Minutes.

W. H. Rodgers was instructed to pay over the collections taken for the American Bible Society, as he had been wont to do.

The Bishop made some most excellent and timely remarks, read the appointments, the doxology was sung, the benediction pronounced, and Conference adjourned *sine die*.

REPORTS.

EDUCATION.

Your committee to whom the subject of Education was referred beg to submit the following report:

The East Tennessee Wesleyan University at Athens, Tennessee, has completed its 13th year of educational life. The past three have been its most prosperous years, its average annual enrollment having been 210. Its body of Alumni are already becoming influential; its scholastic life healthy and vigorous, and its present prospects for students most encouraging. For particulars pertaining to its Faculty, course of study, etc., we beg to refer to its annual catalogue. The report of its trustees show the institution to be free of debt. The income from tuition is wholly inadequate to support the University. But through the efforts of its President its income has been largely supplemented by donations and collections from churches and friends in the North.

The present attendance is larger than usual at this time of the year. Including those now attending and those who will soon return from teaching, there are about 25 young men now preparing for the Ministry. All ministerial students are furnished tuition and text books free. The religious condition of the students is decidedly encouraging. A large number of its students are members of the Sabbath School and its Bible classes. A prayer meeting for the ladies is held at 3 P. M., and one for the gentlemen at 4 P. M., each Sabbath. During the present term a general prayer meeting has been held from 7 to 8 P. M., each Sabbath. Recently these meetings have been seasons of religious power. At present a majority of the advanced students are professors of religion, or are sincerely seeking after the truth.

THE HOLSTON CONFERENCE SEMINARY.

The title to the Holston Conference Seminary property is vested in the Holston Conference for 999 years. It is a clear, unquestioned title. The real estate is valued at $10,000. The institution is now unembarrassed. A small deficiency existing last June at the close of the school, and which was caused by the purchase of lumber, and a balance on current expenses has been so far provided for, that the assets are now quite equal to the liabilities. Some funds have recently been raised by the President in Washington, D. C., and Baltimore, and Wilmington, Delaware. The Rev.

Jeremiah C. Hagey, of Union Church, Washington, D. C., has given the Seminary a No. 1 Estey Chapel Organ, price $275.

Rev. R. Pierce was re-appointed President, and Professor S. P. Fowler, A. B., was appointed last commencement as Principal, and Lucius H. Massey, B. S., as Assistant. Prof. Fowler reports the school in a prosperous condition, with brightening prospects for the future. The enrollment last year was 131 in three departments; of these 23 were music scholars. The past year the grade of the school has been carried up higher than before. Classes were carried through the Freshmen year of regular college course. The moral and religious condition of the school was encouraging. A large portion of the older students were converted the past year. For a full and complete sketch of this Seminary, we refer to the catalogue.

KINGSLEY SEMINARY.

The Kingsley Seminary, situated at Arcadia, Sullivan county, is under the charge of Professor Joseph H. Ketron, A. M., an experienced educator. A new music room and three small houses have recently been added to this property. These improvements have been made largely at the expense of the Principal. They are now occupied by students and parts of families now attending the school. Two more small houses are now in course of construction. The enrollment for the past year was 103. Three students from this Seminary expect to graduate from the East Tennessee Wesleyan University at commencement in 1881.

The departments of Kingsley Seminary seem to be well organized for efficient work. We learn from the Principal that the intellectual improvement of the students has been rapid and substantial. The morals of the school are excellent. Many of the students have been converted and have become active Christian workers. There is a students' prayer meeting every Thursday immediately after the close of the school.

POWELL'S VALLEY SEMINARY.

This institution is well located in the beautiful and fertile valley from which it takes its name. During the past year the trustees have succeeded in completing the building, and at the dedication the entire indebtedness was liquidated. Professor W. A. Wright, A. B., an Alumnus of the East Tennessee Wesleyan University, has been chosen Principal, and now conducts one of the most interesting preparatory schools under the direction of the Conference. The present enrollment is 126. We rejoice in the present prosperity and future prospects of this young institution.

JOHNSON SEMINARY.

This Seminary is located within the bounds of the Chattanooga District, in a wealthy Methodist community. The house has quite recently been refitted and furnished with desks. Rev. M. R. M. Burk, B. S., has been elected Principal for the ensuing year, and the trustees desire his re-appointment by the Holston Conference. The present enrollment is 75.

GREENEVILLE DISTRICT SEMINARY.

This school is situated at Rheatown, and is in charge of Rev. J. C. Wright, A. B., an Alumnus of the East Tennessee Wesleyan University. This property consists of a large two-story brick building, commodiously arranged and well located, and is worth about $3,000; also, a number of fine dormitories belong to the property. The title of this property is vested in the trustees by a 99 years' lease, or so long as it may be occupied for school purposes. Rev. J. C. Wright states that there are 125 enrolled, 60 of whom are large students, and that the prospects of the school are very encouraging. We hereby recommend the appointment of the Rev. J. C. Wright, A. B., as Principal of Greeneville District Seminary.

Your committee would recommend the adoption of the following resolutions:

RESOLVED, 1, That we recommend the appointment of Rev. L. B. Caldwell as Professor of Mineralogy and Geology in the East Tennessee Wesleyan University for the ensuing year.

RESOLVED 2, That we confirm the nomination by the Board of Trustees of the East Tennessee Wesleyan University of Rev. E. Q. Fuller, D. D., Rev. J. S. Petty, C. C. Wester, Esq., E. H. Matthews, Esq., J. W. Ramsey, Esq., Rev. R. S. Rust, D. D., and Bishop H. W. Warren, D. D., as Trustees in the University.

RESOLVED, 3, That we recommend the appointment of Rev. J. W. Mann, M. A. Rule, B. Crist, Professor J. H. Ketron, Professor S. P. Fowler, Revs. T. S. Walker, A. F. Creswell, J. S. Hill, J. A. Ruble, J. F. Perry, W. H. Rodgers, C. B. Sparrow and T. R. West, as Visiting and Examining Committee for the ensuing year.

RESOLVED, 4, That during the Conference year a canvass of the entire territory of the Conference be made under the direction of the President of the University and the Presiding Elders, for the purpose of increasing the number of students in our halls and enlarging the contributions to the University.

All of which is respectfully submitted.

C. B. SPARROW, *Chairman.*

L. B. CALDWELL, *Secretary.*

Greeneville, Tennessee, October 24, 1880.

SUNDAY SCHOOLS.

Your committee report as follows: We are more than ever impressed with the value, importance and magnitude of the Sunday School work. We therefore offer the following resolutions:

1. That during the ensuing year we will try to carry out the *letter* and *spirit* of the discipline on Sunday Schools.

2. That we will use all of our influence in supplying all of our Sunday Schools with our own literature, believing it to be the best for Methodist Sunday Schools.

3. That we will introduce and use in all of our schools our Catechisms.

4. That we will, as far as possible, organize all of our Sunday Schools into Missionary Societies, and will hold regular Sunday School missionary meetings.

5. That we recommend all of our Presiding Elders to organize their districts into normal institutes, and hold in connection with the District Conference a session, devoting one entire day to this work.

6. That we request each of the pastors to hold sometime during the year a Sunday School Convention on each charge.

7. That we will all, without fail, take the annual collection for the Sunday School Union, and will put forth vigorous efforts to meet the assessments.

A. J. GREER,

F. H. HODGE,

J. B. FORD.

TEMPERANCE.

Intemperance is one of the most potent enemies of both church and state. It arrays itself against every principle of right and economy; it antagonizes everything that tends to bless and ennoble humanity. The entire history of the liquor traffic is fraught with every specie of crime and grade of affliction that mars the purity and happiness of the human race. It costs the State of Tennessee twenty-six millions dollars annually, more than enough to liquidate the entire State debt. Two-thirds of all our paupers and criminals are the fruits of this unholy traffic. Strewn along the path of this fell destroyer may be found a large per centage of all the vicious. insane and wretchedly demoralized of our land. and yet our State legalizes a traffic that is productive of all this deplorable wretchedness. It is impossible to exaggerate the evils of intemperance. or over-state the moral criminality and inexcusableness of the liquor traffic, and so long as the business is popularized by being legalized. so long will we be powerless to stop or suppress it. Moral suasion shuts up no saloon. and has but a feeble force to reclaim the youthful inebriate: therefore.

RESOLVED, That we recommend by memorial to the General Assembly of the State of Tennessee the passage of a Local Option Law, and that the memorial be signed by the President and Secretary of this body.

2. That we recommend the formation of temperance societies in all our charges, to receive signers of men and women to memorials to be sent to the Legislature praying for the passage of a Local Option Law.

J. F. SPENCE, Chairman.

AMERICAN BIBLE SOCIETY.

The Committee on Bible Cause report that since our last annual meeting thousands of families have been supplied, in whole or in part, with the Holy Scriptures, and yet it is a lamentable fact that within the bounds of the Holston Conference there are thousands of families still destitute of this precious treasure.

The American Bible Society, during the past year, has nobly responded to our calls in supplying us with the Word of God, and still promises to meet all the demands made on her; to supply all the people, without regard to race or color. In view of the noble christian liberality of the American Bible Society, not only to us and our nation, but to many nations, we therefore renew our resolution as adopted by our Conference for several years past, that we will take a collection in all our pastoral charges for the Bible cause.

RESOLVED, That we request the appointment of Rev. W. H. Rodgers as Bible Colporteur for the ensuing year.

Respectfully submitted.
W. H. RODGERS, Chairman.

CHURCH EXTENTION.

The obligation upon the strong to help the weak is from God, and is imperative, and applies to furnishing places of worship, as well as any other necessity, and we regard the meeting house as indispensable to the spread of the Gospel and the speedy conversion of the world. We renew our thanksgiving to God and acknowledge our obligation to the Church

Extension Society for the work done in general, and especially for the aid afforded this Conference. We would renew our devotion to this cause, promising greater diligence in the diffusion of intelligence, and greater earnestness in pressing the collections during the coming year: and to this end we recommend that all our preachers who are not supplied already with such helps as are given gratuitously by the Church Extension Board, apply at once and procure the means of information, and that at least one sermon or lecture be given to each society in our charges during the year.

Respectfully submitted,
S. TINKER, Chairman.

EPISCOPAL FUND.

WHEREAS, Our beloved Bishops are very active, faithful and efficient; therefore,

RESOLVED, 1. That we pledge ourselves to meet promptly and fully the $188 assessed this Conference for their support.

RESOLVED, 2. That the Presiding Elders be instructed to apportion this amount to the districts and charges and early in the year publish the same.

RESOLVED, 3. That the amounts raised be published in the Minutes with the benevolent collections next year.

J. M. DURHAM,
R. PIERCE,
WM. KINSLAND.

TRACTS.

Believing that a judicious distribution of tracts greatly facilitates the work of spreading the gospel, therefore,

RESOLVED, That we believe our tracts to be most excellent and helpful in supplementing our pulpit and pastoral efforts, and we call special attention to the variety of tracts furnished by our Tract Society, and to their adaptation to the necessities of the age. We also strongly recommend that both the Pastors and the Tract Committees, appointed by the Quarterly Conferences, engage in this work.

RESOLVED, That we will take the collection in all our charges.

J. S. HILL, Chairman.

CHURCH LITERATURE.

Believing that a wider circulation of our Church Literature would very greatly assist in the prosecution of our work, we would call special attention to the following:

1st. We recommend that as many of our preachers as can subscribe for *The Quarterly Review*—a magazine of the highest theological excellence.

2d. *The Methodist Advocate*, published at Atlanta, a paper that has done more for the advancement of our work in the South than all the other papers of our Church—a fearless defender of right. It ought to have twice as large a circulation as it has, and we as members of the Holston Conference pledge ourselves to do all we can to double its circulation in the bounds of our Conference, believing that it has a claim upon our effort before any other religious paper.

We cheerfully endorse the *Advocate* and its editor. Rev. E. Q. Fuller, D. D.

Respectfully submitted.

J. B. FORD, *Chairman.*

AUDITING COMMITTEE.

We have carefully examined the accounts of the Presiding Elders of the different districts and find them correct.

SAMUEL GREEAR,
M. A. RULE,
M. WILLIAMS.

GREENEVILLE, Oct. 20. 1880.

THE CASE OF H. H. BURK.

From the facts before us it appears that Bro. Burk was greatly provoked and suffered himself to be drawn into a personal difficulty.

RESOLVED, Therefore, that while we allow that he was very provokingly insulted, we disapprove of his conduct as being beneath the dignity and high standard of moral excellence and self possession that ought to characterize the ministers of our Lord Jesus Christ, and that we recommend that he be reprimanded by the presiding Bishop.

Respectfully submitted.

D. RICHARDSON,
S. GREEAR,
J. F. PERRY.

CONFERENCE RECORD.

We have examined the records of the Knoxville, Cleveland and Russellville Districts, and the Tennessee part of the Asheville District Conference, and find them correct and in disciplinary form. From Powell's Valley, Greeneville, Chattanooga and Kingston Districts, no records were presented to the Committee.

JOHN F. SPENCE, *Chairman.*

REPORT OF THE COMMITTEE ON THE FREEDMEN'S AID SOCIETY.

We fully recognize the magnitude and great importance of the work of the Freedmen's Aid Society. This cannot better be presented than in the language of the last Annual Report:

"The work of elevating a race, brought out of heathenism, degraded by superstition and vice, and reared under the influences of slavery is a gigantic one. It cannot be accomplished by the fitful efforts of a few years; protracted effort, unfaltering faith, and money in large installments are essential to its achievement. Those who at first regarded this enterprise as temporary, and expected to be relieved of the burden at an early day, have changed their views, as they have come to realize how vast a work, in the providence of God has been thrust upon us, how great has been the success in its prosecutions, and how intimately it is connected with the permanence of our free institutions and the purity and prosperity of our Church in the South.

"The important work of the American church, and the one that urges its claims with peculiar emphasis at this crisis, is that of educating the freedmen. God places this duty upon us as he does on no other nation, and he will not receive work done in any other part of the world as an equivalent for our neglect of this which is so imperatively demanded in our own country. To neglect it, or to treat it with cold indifference, is to put in jeopardy one of the most momentous interests intrusted to the church and the nation. This cause, at this hour, has transcendent claims upon us, and whatever other work we may postpone or neglect in the world's redemption, we cannot innocently turn away from this movement in behalf of the freedmen, which is so closely identified with the welfare of this country and the salvation of the world."

Only a few of our people have a true appreciation of the greatness of the the work undertaken by this society, the urgency of its claims, and opportunity it presents of accomplishing grand results with a moderate expenditure.   Take into consideration the variety, the scope, and extent of this educational enterprise, one medical college, three theological schools, six chartered universities and colleges, ten seminaries and boarding schools, centrally located in important positions in the South, and you may get some slight conception of the vastness of the work undertaken and the favorable opportunity afforded in it for the Christian *co-operation and liberal* investment.   We are clear in our conviction that this work for the freedmen should be carried on with increased activity and enlarged liberality.   The action of the late General Conference in regard to the education of our poorer white population makes it our duty to consider this new departure also.   The Bishops in their quadrennial address, after speaking of the Freedmen's work say: "We deem it also of great importance that a similar work should be done among the white members and friends in the South."

Possibly the sphere of the Freedmen's Aid Society might be enlarged so that it would work in the same lines in this field also.   At all events the educational work among the poorer white people of the South should be in some way developed through the general benevolence of the church.

The General Conference took the following action:

Resolved, 1. That under the phrase "and others," of Article Second, in the Constitution of the Freedmen's Aid Society, we see the way clear to aid the schools which have been established by our church in the Southern States among the white people, and hereby recommend to the board of managers of this society, to give such aid to these schools during the next quadrennium as can be done without embarrassment to the schools among the Freedmen.

Resolved, 2. That our pastors in presenting the claims of the society to the church should remind our people that a portion of the appropriations of the society will be made for the education of the white population connected with our church in the Southern States; but not to the embarrassment of the work among our people of color.

The above broad comprehensive action was taken by the General Conference.   We rejoice to be able to say that this action, in our judgment, is in accord with the sentiment and wishes of the church.   We have facts before us that convince us that the Methodist Episcopal Church would contribute annually $50,000 if the facts and wants of our schools for the whites were placed fully and clearly before them.

2. And we fully indorse the proposition of the Freedmen's Aid Society to increase the fund of said society for the coming year to $125,000, and hereby pledge the co-operation of the Holston Conference, to the best of its ability to raise the sum of $700 apportioned to it for that purpose.

3. And we deem it indispensable that a strong personal presentation of the white work be made, and we earnestly request that the Board of the

Freedmen's Aid Society, at its earliest convenience, put at least two efficient men into the field to bring this matter before the Conferences and churches of the North.

4. And your committee further suggest that the Holston Conference memorialize the Conferences of the South, yet to be held this year, to join with us in the above request to the Board of the Freedmen's Aid Society.

       Respectfully submitted.

G. W. HENINGER,
J. F. JENNINGS,
D. B. LAWTON,
L. B. CALDWELL,
R. PIERCE.

CONFERENCE STEWARD'S REPORT.

CHARGES.	PREACHERS	SALARIES.			CONFERENCE CLAIMANTS.
		ESTIMATED.	RECEIVED.	DEFICIT.	
KNOXVILLE DISTRICT...	J. A. Ruble........	$900 00	$787 25	$112 75	.....
Knoxville, 1st Charge....	C. B. Sparrow.....	1,200 50	1,200 00	....	$4 50
Knoxville, 2d Charge.....	J. M. Durham.....	·500 00	369 11	130 89	50
Knox Circuit.............	J. B. Little........	400 00	300 00	100 00	20 00
Campbell Station........	P. H. Henry......	300 00	154 00	146 00	4 00
Thorn Grove............	J. B. Seaton.......	300 00	129 00	171 00	1 50
Little River.............	W. C. Graves......	450 00	231 80	218 20	8 83
Sevierville..............	E. B. Clark.......	430 00	430 00	....	5 00
Fair Garden.............	D. S. Hodsden	330 00	182 80	147 20	1 75
New Market.............	{ J. H. Jennings, { R. Pierce...... }	400 00	335 23	64 77	2 00
Maryville...............	J. D. Lawson......	400 00	245 00	155 00	7 56
Madisonville	J. N. Moore.......	300 00	150 95	149 05	85
Loudon..................	T. H. Hodge......	350 00	200 00	150 00	2 00
Total..............		6,260 00	4,715 14	1,544 86	58 49
POWELL'S VALLEY DIST.	T. S. Walker.......	700 00	445 56	254 44	.....
Fincastle	Jas. Annis	225 00	17 25	207 75	.....
Jacksborough	A. G. Watkins.....	400 00	65 00	335 00	.....
Clinton	B. Crist...........	400 00	244 54	155 46	1 50
Huntsville...............	J. Forrister........				1 00
Clear Fork & Speedwell...	G. W. Jarvis.......	315 00	170 45	144 55	1 00
Tazewell................	Wm. M Haskell....	250 00	96 50	153 50	1 00
Thorn Hill..............	L. Bogart.........	260 00	80 00	180 00	1 00
Maynardville............	Wm. Kinsland.....	250 00	125 00	125 00	.....
Rutledge................	W. T. Senter.......	350 00	187 00	163 00	.....
Speedville	H. Pyle...........				
Big Valley..............	A. J. Greer........	400 00	147 87	252 13	25
Rogersville.............	M. A. Rule........	300 00	172 00	128 00	1 25
Total..............		3,850 00	1,751 17	2,098 83	7 00
GREENEVILLE DIST.....	J. W. Mann.......	624 00	566 00	50 00	.....
Greeneville..............	J. J. Manker......	600 00	600 00	....	1 00
Greeneville Circuit.......	T. B. Russell......	350 00	327 00	23 00	2 00
Rheatown	J. L. Cardwell.....				1 00
St. Clair................	M. Seaton.........	350 00	323 31	26 69	1 25
Fall Branch.............	A. J. Bruner......	400 00	300 00	100 00	1 00
Jonesboro'..............	J. D. Roberson....	330 00	281 18	48 82	50
Elizabethton	G. W. Heninger...	300 00	300 00	....	.....
Johnson City............	J. R. Hughes......	395 00	305 00	90 00	1 00
Taylorsville.............	C. D. Munsey......	300 00	255 00	45 00	1 00
Kingsport...............	J. P Milburn......	300 00	256 30	43 70	3 00
Irvin...................	R. C. Robertson...				
Telford	{ J. R. Shultz.... { I. C. Patton.... }	400 00	206 65	193 35	10
Total..............		4,349 00	3,720 44	628 56	11 85
ASHEVILLE DIST........	W. C. Daily.......	500 00	492 00	8 00	.....
Parrottsville............	T. W. Brown......	230 00	210 00	20 00	3 05
Morristown....:.......	T. R. West........	340 00	228 00	112 00	2 15
Mossy Creek............	P. H. Reed........	150 00	100 00	50 00	50
Total..............		1,220 00	1,030 00	190 00	5 70

Conference Steward's Report--Continued

| CHARGES. | PREACHERS. | SALARIES. | | | CONFERENCE CLAIMANTS. |
		ESTIMATED.	RECEIVED.	DEFICIT.	
CHATTANOOGA DIST.....	J. S. Petty..........	$650 00	$550 00	$100 00	.....
Chattanooga.............	S. Tinker............	760 00	760 00	....	$8 00
Ooltewah..............	J. A. Baker........	250 00	243 73	6 27	1 00
Cleveland.............	J. S. Hill............	300 00	300 00	....	6 50
Cleveland Circuit........	E. M. Lockwood...	400 00	350 00	50 00	3 00
Chatata................	R. O. Ayers........	360 00	330 00	30 00	7 00
Sewee................	Geo. Julian........	200 00	167 00	33 00	4 00
Athens...............	L. B. Caldwell....	....	25 00	....	3 31
Athens Circuit..........	G. W. Coleman....	225 00	200 00	25 00	1 60
Bine Springs.............	G. M. Stone.......	245 00	169 00	76 00	4 00
Ducktown	W. R. Long........	....	....	....	85
Murphy...............	R. M. Witt........	....	....	....	.....
Total............		3,390 00	3,094 73	320 27	39 26
KINGSTON DISTRICT....	T. H. Russell.......	525 00	513 40	11 60	.....
Kingston and Rockwood.	J. C. Wright.......	200 00	200 00	....	1 00
Kingston Circuit..........	H. H. Burk........	....	....	....	1 00
Scarborough.............	S. Greear........	260 00	138 00	122 00	.....
Wartburg...............	A. C. Peters.......	....	....	....	.....
Jamestown.............	S. B. Scott........	....	....	....	.....
Crossville.............	J. W. Burnett.....	250 00	144 00	106 00	50
Pikeville	J. J. Robinett.....	210 00	100 00	110 00	50
Hamilton.............	D. Richardson....	200 00	161 96	38 04	1 00
Dayton...............	J. F. Perry........	201 00	201 00	....	50
Jasper	J. A. Nicholson....	250 00	160 00	90 00	5 00
Battle Creek...........	T. A. Cass........	....	....	....	.....
Cumberland...........	J. C. Tate........	....	....	....	.....
Total............		2,096 00	1,618 36	477 64	9 50
CLEVELAND DIST.......	J. S. Harris........	850 00	667 77	182 23	.....
Chattanooga.............	M. Williams.......	650 00	650 00	....	4 00
Marion...............	J. W. Woods......	300 00	93 00	207 00	25
Chattanooga Circuit.....	J. W. Wells	250 00	60 00	190 00	10
Washington	J. Mann..........	336 00	65 00	271 00	60
Kingston	H. N. Brown......	300 00	124 95	175 05	35
McDonald.............	G. N. Johnson.....	250 00	75 00	175 00	10
Bradley...............	B. C. Johnson.....	260 00	87 00	173 00	25
Soddy................	A. Douglas........	350 00	185 00	165 00	50
Knoxville	O. N. Hypsher	300 00	75 50	224 50	50
Ebenezer	W. S. Marley.....	300 00	66 00	234 00	1 00
Robertsville		....	....	....	.....
Bleeville	Clemm Shaw.....	300 00	86 55	213 45	10
Total.		4,446 00	2,235 77	2,210 23	7 05
RUSSELLVILLE DIST.....	C. K. Mays........	200 00	100 00	100 00	.....
Limestone	B. Williams.......	200 00	40 00	160 00	.....
Midway...............	W. Mill............	150 00	39 00	111 00	25
Sevierville	A. Jordan.........	100 00	44 00	56 00	25
Hawkins.............	C. Boyd..........	100 00	50 00	50 00	.....
Mineral Hill.............	H. Jones..........	120 00	36 00	64 00	10
Coal Creek...........	A. J. Fletcher.....	250 00	118 00	132 00	25
Watauga...............	W. Bluford.......	275 00	200 00	75 00	50
Russellville.............	Alex Gillespie.....	150 00	80 00	70 00	50
Total............		1,545 00	707 00	818 00	1 85

REPORT OF THE TREASURER.

OF THE CONFERENCE BOARD OF THE CHURCH EXTENSION FOR THE YEAR
ENDING OCTOBER, 1880.

KNOXVILLE DISTRICT.

Knoxville 1st Church.........$15 00
Knox circuit.....................	3 00
Mew Market......................	50
Maryville	1 00
Loudon...........................	50
Campbell Station...............	50
Thorn Grove....................	25
Little River....................	1 62
	22 37

GREENEVILLE DISTRICT.

Greeneville......................	2 00
Greeneville circuit..............	2 25
Fall Branch.....................	50
St. Clair........................	1 00
Johnson City....................	5 00
Kingsport.	50
Rheatown circuit...............	50
	11 75

CHATTANOOGA DISTRICT.

Chattanooga..	10 00
Cleveland........................	4 00
Cleveland circuit...............	2 00
Ooltewah	1 70
Chatata..........................	4 00
Blue Spring.....................	75
Ducktown........................	1 30
	23 75

KINGSTON DISTRICT.

Kingston station................	3 00
Jasper circuit...................	1 00
Pikeville circuit................	50
	4 50

POWELL'S VALLEY DISTRICT.

Rogersville circuit.............$ 1 05
Clinton circuit..................	1 00
Huntsville circuit...............	50
Speedwell circuit......	50
Thorn Hill......................	25
	3 30

ASHEVILLE DISTRICT

Morristown circuit............	20
Parrottsville circuit............	50
Newport circuit.................	50
Mossy Creek circuit...........	50
	1 70

CLEVELAND DISTRICT.

Chattanooga	15 00
Marion circuit..................	25
McDonald circuit...............	15
Kingston circuit................	50
Washington circuit............	50
Riceville circuit................	20
Chattanooga circuit..	1 00
Soddy circuit...................	1 50
Bradley circuit..................	55
Ebenezer circuit................	1 75
Knoxville	1 00
Robertsville....................	15
	22 55

RUSSELLVILLE DISTRICT.

Russellville circuit.	50
Midway circuit..................	25
Mineral Hill circuit............	25
Wautaga circuit................	1 00
Sevierville circuit..............	25
Hawkins circuit.............. .	20
	2 45

RECAPITULATION.

Knoxville District. $22 37
Greeneville District..	11 75
Chattanooga District...	23 75
Kingston District..	4 50
Powell's Valley District...	3 30
Asheville District...	1 70
Cleveland District.................:.................................	22 55
Russellville District...	2 45
	$92 37

October 20, 1880.   J. J. MANKER, *Treasurer.*

MISSIONS.

KNOXVILLE DISTRICT........$125 00	CHATTANOOGA DISTRICT.....$180 00
Knoxville 2d Church.......... 170 00	Ooltewah 20 00
Newport 20 00	Cleveland station.............. 85 00
Fair Garden................... 45 00	Cleveland circuit.............. 40 00
Thorn Grove.................. 20 00	Sewee...................... .. 20 00
	Blue Spring.................... 40 00
Total.....................$380 00	Athens station................. 240 00
	Athens circuit................. 25 00
POWELL'S VALLEY DISTRICT. $220 00	Ducktown...................... 100 00
Jacksboro' 60 00	Madisonville.................. 40 00
Clinton 35 00	
Tazewell....................... 30 00	Total.....................$790 00
Thorn Hill..................... 45 00	
Big Valley. 50 00	KINGSTON DISTRICT.... .....$200 00
Maynardville 55 00	Crossville 50 00
Rogersville..................... 20 00	Jamestown..................... 50 00
Morristown.................... 35 00	Wartburg...................... 50 00
Rutledge....................... 30 00	Scarborough.................. 40 00
	Battle Creek. 40 00
Total..................... $580 00	Kingston...................... 60 00·
	Kingston circuit.............. 100 00
GREENEVILLE DISTRICT......$140 00	Rugby and Huntsville. 100 00
Greeneville.................... 90 00	
Jonesboro' 50 00	Total.....................$690 00
Jonesboro' circuit............. 50 00	
Elizabethton.................. 40 00	Grand Total...............$2,900 00
Ervin........................... 50 00	
Johnson City circuit......... 100 00	
Parrottsville.................. 40 00	
Total.....................$560 00	

I concur in the above appropriations.

E. O. HAVEN, *President.*

October 24, 1880.

RESOLUTIONS.

BISHOP HAVEN.

Resolved, That Bishop E. O. Haven, by his kind, courteous bearing, his faithful and patient attention to all matters of business, his wise and godly administration, and his able addresses merit not only our confidence and respect, but our affection, and we most cordially invite him to visit us again.

J. F. SPENCE.

THANKS.

Resolved, That Rev. J. W. Mann and Rev. J. J. Manker, for their careful provision for our comfort, the citizens of Greeneville for their cordial and bountiful entertainment of the members of the Conference, and the East Tennessee and Georgia Railroad for excursion rates, are all entitled to our sincere and hearty thanks which we hereby most cordially tender.

J. F. SPENCE.

COLLECTIONS.

Resolved, That our collections be taken in the same order as last year.

C. B. SPARROW.

CONFERENCE CLAIMANTS.

Whereas, There is a growing disposition on the part of this Conference to provide more liberally for the wants of our worn-out preachers, their widows and orphans; therefore,

Resolved, That the Stewards ascertain the amount necessary for a comfortable support of our Conference claimants and apportion the same to the several districts, and that the Presiding Elders assess the same to their several charges. And, be it further

Resolved, That each preacher at the next Conference embody in his report the amount of his collection for Conference claimants, and also the amount assessed his charge.

C. B. SPARROW,
J. F. SPENCE.

CONFERENCE RELATIONS.

RESOLVED, That the Presiding Elders be, and they hereby are instructed to refer to the Committee on Conference Relations the names of such persons in their districts, as in their judgment should engage the attention of the Committee, with such recommendation as they may think proper in each case, at least six weeks before the next session.

RESOLVED, That the Committee shall not be held as under obligation to consider the relation of any parties whose names have not been referred to them as above.

J. J. MANKER.

STATE REFORM SCHOOL.

WHEREAS. There has been a strong effort on the part of many of the leading citizens of the State of Tennessee to establish a State Reform School for homeless youths: therefore,

RESOLVED, That we, the members of the Holston Conference, are in hearty sympathy with the enterprise and will do all we can to aid it.

J. F. SPENCE,
C. B. SPARROW.

THE CHOIR.

RESOLVED, That our thanks are due and are hereby tendered the Choir for the most excellent music furnished during the session of the Conference.

J. A. RUBLE.

TRUSTEES AT JOHNSON CITY.

WHEREAS. A few of our brethren as a Board of Trustees of the parsonage property of Jonesboro' circuit have been involved in a long and costly law suit which was finally lost, leaving said Board of Trustees. by judgment of the court, legally responsible for about eight hundred dollars: and,

WHEREAS, These brethren have given their time, money and labor in the interests of the church; therefore,

RESOLVED, That we sympathize with the brethren, and feel that as a

Conference we ought to bring this matter before all our congregations and ask them to assist in liquidating this debt.

RESOLVED, That we will bring this matter before all our congregations during January, and do what we can in raising money to satisfy the judgment against the above trustees.

RESOLVED, That the Presiding Elders be instructed to see that this collection is taken at the time indicated.

J. A. RUBLE,
J. W. MANN,
J. R. HUGHES.

NEW CONFERENCE.

RESOLVED, By the Holston Annual Conference of the Methodist Episcopal Church in Annual Session assembled, that it is the sense of this body that the highest and best interests of both races will be more speedily and more certainly secured and promoted by separate Conference organizations.

RESOLVED, That the colored portion of our work be, and with the concurrence of the Presiding Bishop, is hereby constituted a separate and distinct body, under the name and designation of the East Tennessee Conference of the Methodist Episcopal Church.

RESOLVED, That as an indication of our interest in the new Conference, and that we may do all that is possible for its success, two thousand dollars of the missionary appropriation to the Holston Conference be, and is hereby set aside for the support of the work in the East Tennessee Conference.

GREENEVILLE, TENN., October 23, 1880.

Unanimously adopted by a rising vote.

MEMOIRS.

MRS. JULIA TARBELL MANKER.

JULIA TARBELL MANKER, wife of Rev. John J. Manker, A. M., of the Holston Annual Conference, was born in Ripley, Ohio, February 8, 1841, and died at the parsonage of the Methodist Episcopal Church, in Greeneville, Tennessee, September 21, 1880. Her disease was pulmonary consumption. She suffered long—she suffered much, but was pre-eminently resigned in affliction and triumphant in death. In life and in death she was one of the purest, brightest and best of earth. She combined in her character the distinguishing graces and virtues which make the human life divine.

Having been trained by deeply pious parents in the service of the ever-loving and altogether lovely Jesus, she became, early in life, not only an amiable and pious student, but an accomplished and efficient teacher. She was married September 9, 1863, and soon thereafter came South with her faithful husband to seek for a field of Christain usefulness among strangers.

Through all these years she has been well known and greatly beloved in Knoxville, Athens and Greeneville—prominent stations in Holston Conference—as a devoted wife, loving mother, faithful friend and model Christian.

After appropriate and impressive funeral services, attended by a large concourse of citizens and friends, and conducted by Revs. J. B. Ford, J. W. Mann, C. B. Sparrow and J. A. Ruble, in the First Methodist Episcopal Church of Knoxville, Tenn., the loved form of the departed was bequeathed to the guardianship of the grave, in Gray Cemetery, of that city.

> " Yet not thus buried or extinct,
> The vital spark shall lie ;
> For o'er life's wreck that spark shall rise
> To seek its kindred sky."

O, may the husband, four sons and only daughter meet the wife and mother, with the angel babe, in the bright forever and city of our God.

J. W. MANN,
J. B. FORD.
W. C. DAILY.

MRS. SARAH ANN JENNINGS.

Mrs. Sarah Ann, wife of Rev. J. H. Jennings, of Holston Conference (Methodist Episcopal Church), died April 20, 1880, at her home in New Market, Tenn. Sister Jennings was born in 1821, in Blount county, Tenn., where she was also raised. In her 16th year she was converted, and united with the Methodist Episcopal Church, of which she remained a faithful member until she fell asleep in Christ. She and brother Jennings were united in marriage in 1860. Some four years ago the deceased was stricken with paralysis. Some eighteen months ago she had a second stroke, from which she never rallied, but remained almost entirely helpless, until the long looked for third attack came. This occurred Tuesday morning, April 20th, at 6 a. m. From this she never aroused, but lay speechless, and apparently unconscious, until 4 p. m., when her earth-weary but glad spirit went home to heaven. During all her protracted affliction, she manifested wonderful patience to the Lord's will. Never did she murmur or seem to "wish her sufferings less." She was a woman of cultivated mind and of deep, solid piety, adorning the different relations of life as becometh the Gospel of the Saviour. As the wife of an itinerant Methodist preacher, she was subject to the sacrifices, hardships and burdens peculiar thereto, and in this country they are neither few nor light, but many and grievous, crushing many a spirit and spreading a shadow of aching sadness over many a heart. But this good woman was ever ready to make sacrifices and endure the privations incident to our itinerancy, ever cheering and encouraging her husband in his "work of faith and labor of love," never saying "stay," but, though sick and helpless, and for years needing a husband's constant presence and care, she would bid him go to his appointment, saying, "The Lord will take care of me." Strong ties bound her to earth; with these doubtless she would fain have stayed, but still stronger attractions drew her longing heart heavenward, for not only kindred dear, but Christ was there, and seemed to beckon her away, so she had a strong "desire to depart and be with Christ, which is far better," saying were it not for the dear home ties of husband and son, she would not turn her hand to live. There was no struggle in her death, it seemed to be painless, sinking softly as an infant drops to sleep, or as a summer cloud melts away. Her funeral was held in the Methodist Episcopal Church in the presence of a large concourse of sympathising people, and conducted by Prof. R. Pierce and the writer. She leaves a husband, two children, three brothers and three sisters, to mourn, but thank God, "not as those who have no hope." May our kind heavenly Father bless and comfort the bereaved ones!

W. C. DAILY.

New Market, Tenn., May 4, 1880.

EAST TENNESSEE
ANNUAL CONFERENCE,

GREENEVILLE, TENNESSEE,

OCTOBER 25, 1880.

PROCEEDINGS.

The East Tennessee Annual Conference held its first session in Greeneville, Tennessee, October 25th, 1880, which met at the Greeneville Methodist Episcopal Church (colored), at 9 o'clock A. M., with Bishop E. O. Haven presiding. S. J. Harris conducting the religious services, and prayer by Wm. Bluford. after which B. H. Johnson was elected Secretary.

The roll was called and the following members answered to their names:

C. K. Mays, S. J. Harris, D. B. Lawton, Wm. Bluford, Wm. H. Rogers, Wm. M. Haskell, W. C. Graves, A. J. Fletcher, O. N. Hypshire, Alexander Jordan, Wm. Mills and Alexander Gillespie.

The following members were absent: J. C. Tate, J. W. Wells, Jas. Yarnell, Alex. Lindsay and C. Shaw.

DISCIPLINARY QUESTIONS.

1. *Who are received by transfer, and from What Conference?*
Miles Williams, from the Tennessee Conference.

2. *Who are admitted on trial?*
B. H. Johnson, J. Tate and Wm. T. Marley.

3. *Who remain on trial?*
Chas. Boyd. H. N. Brown, A. Douglass. H. Jones and M. Williams.

4. *Who are discontinued?*
B. Williams.

5. *Who are admitted into full connection?*
Jos. W. Wells.

6. *Who are re-admitted?*
Jas. Yarnell.

7. *Who are received on credentials from other churches?*
A. Lindsay and Wm. Mills.

8. *What traveling preachers have been elected Deacons?*
None.

9. *What traveling preachers have been ordained Deacons?*
None.

10. *What local preachers have been elected Deacons?*
A. Douglass, L. Cobb, H. N. Brown, B. H. Johnson and Alex. Gillespie.

11. *What local preachers have been ordained Deacons?*
All that were elected.

12. *Who are the traveling Deacons of the first class?*
None.

13. *Who are the traveling Deacons of the second class?*
A. J. Fletcher, O. N. Hypshire and Alexander Jordan.

14. *What traveling Deacons have been elected elders?*
None.

15. *What traveling Deacons have been ordained elders?*
None.

16. *What local Deacons have been elected elders?*
None.

17. *What local Deacons have been ordained elders?*
None.

18. *Who are the supernumerary preachers?*
There are none.

19. *Who are the superannuated preachers?* .
C. K. Mays.

20. *Was the character of each preacher examined?*
It was.

21. *Have any died?*
None.

22. *Have any been transferred, and to what Conference?*
A. P. Melton to Savannah Conference, Georgia.

23. *Have any withdrawn?*
None.

24. *Have any located at their own request?*
J. Mann.

25. *Have any been located?*
None.

26. *Have any been permitted to withdraw under charge?*
None.

27 *Have any been expelled?*
None.

28. *Who are Triers of Appeals?*
C. K. Mays, S. J. Harris, D. B. Lawton, Wm. Bluford. Wm.
H. Rogers, Wm. M. Haskell and W. C. Graves.

29. *What is the Statistical Report for this year?*
[See statistical tables.]

30. *What are the claims on the Conference fund?*
This was not answered.

31. *What has been received on these claims. and how has it been applied?*
Twenty dollars, distributed according to the order of the Conference.

32. *Where are the preachers stationed?*
[See appointments.]

33. *Where shall the next Conference be held?*
At Clinton, Tennessee.

— ·

On motion D. B. Lawton's relation was changed from superannuated to effective.

At his request C. K. Mays was made a superannuate.

The Bishop appointed S. J. Harris to preach the Missionary sermon at next Conference, and W. H. Rogers alternate.

On motion a Committee to nominate the various Examining Committees was appointed. consisting of Wm. M. Haskell. O. N. Hypshire and A. J. Fletcher, who reported as follows: (See committees.)

The Bishop nominated the following as a Conference Board of Church Extension: Mr. Geo. W. Sewell, President; Wm· H. Rogers. Vice-President; R. Howard. Treasurer; B. H. Johnson, Secretary.

The Missionary appropriations were read (see report), which was adopted. subject to any modification the Presiding Elders may see cause to make, with the approval of the Presiding Bishop.

On motion the following resolution was offered:

RESOLVED, That it is the sense of this Conference that all of the property now occupied by the East Tennessee Annual Conference shall be set apart for the use of said Conference.

On motion it was

RESOLVED, That the Bishop be requested to present our necessities to the Missionary Committee and Board of Church Extension at their next meeting.

J. S. Hill, Statistical Secretary, read his report, which was approved.

On motion it was

RESOLVED, That the Minutes of the East Tennessee Conference be published with the Minutes of the Holston Conference.

S. J. Harris offered the following resolution:

RESOLVED, That the thanks of this Conference are hereby tendered our beloved Bishop, E. O. Haven, for the kind manner in which he has presided over our Conference, and we earnestly ask and pray for his return again in our midst. Also, to Bishop H. W. Warren for the kind words we received and the concern he expressed in our behalf.

On motion it was

RESOLVED, That all of the candidates for examination come before the Committees on the day previous to the day of the next Conference, at 6:30 o'clock. P. M.

Quite a number of our best white friends were present at the organization of our Conference. Dr. E. Q. Fuller, of Atlanta, Ga., made a few remarks in the interest of our new Conference; also in interest of the *Atlanta Methodist Advocate*, and several subscribed for the paper.

Dr. J. M. Freeman, of New York, Corresponding Secretary of the Sunday School Union, addressed the members of the Conference upon the importance of supplying our Methodist Sunday Schools with the literature of our own publishing houses, also Tract Society.

The Bishop made a very good impression upon those present in his closing remarks, after which the appointments were read, and we were led in prayer by C. K. Mays.

The Minutes were read and approved, the doxology was sung, and the Conference adjourned with benediction by Bishop Haven.

B. H. JOHNSON, *Secretary*.

APPOINTMENTS.

CHATTANOOGA DISTRICT.

S. J. HARRIS, P. E.	P. O. Chattanooga, Tenn., box 217.
Chattanooga station.	M. Williams.
Chattanooga circuit.	C. Shaw.
Cleveland circuit.	B. H. Johnson.
Cumberland.	J. C. Tate.
Ebenezer.	Alex. Lindsay.
Kingston	H. N. Brown.
Knoxville	(W. T. Marley,
	(D. B. Lawton.
McDonald	Jas. Yarnell.
Marion	A. Douglass.
Riceville	(To be supplied).
Robertsville.	(To be supplied).
Soddy.	O. N. Hypshire.
Washington	J. W. Wells.

Wm. H. Rogers, Agent of the American Bible Society and member of the Cleveland Quarterly Conference.

MORRISTOWN DISTRICT.

W. C. GRAVES, P. E.	P. O. Morristown, Tenn.
Coal Creek circuit.	A. J. Fletcher.
Doe River.	Charles Boyd.
Greeneville.	(To be supplied).
Hawkins.	J. C. Tate.
Horse Creek.	(To be supplied).
Limestone.	Henry Jones.
Midway.	Wm. Mills.
Mineral Hill.	Wm. Bluford.
New River.	(To be supplied).
Russellville.	A. Gillespie.
Sevierville.	A. Jordan.

Wm. M. Haskell, Sunday-school Agent and evangelical member of the Russellville Quarterly Conference.

MISSIONARY APPROPRIATIONS.

CHATTANOOGA DISTRICT.

S. J. HARRIS, P. E.		$250 00
Chattanooga circuit	C. Shaw	40 00
Cleveland circuit	B. H. Johnson	65 00
Ebenezer circuit.?	A. Lindsay	40 00
Kingston circuit	II. N. Brown	65 00
Knoxville	{W. T. Marley	70 00
	{D. B. Lawton	200 00
McDonald circuit	Jas. Yarnell	40 00
Marion circuit	A. Douglass	50 00
Riceville circuit	(To be supplied)	47 50
Robertsville circuit	(To be supplied)	35 00
Soddy circuit	O. N. Hypshire	47 50
Washington circuit	J. W. Wells	45 00
W. H. Rogers, Bible Agent		25 00

MORRISTOWN DISTRICT.

W. C. GRAVES, P. E.		$250 00
Coal Creek circuit	A. J. Fletcher	50 00
Doe River circuit	C. Boyd	40 00
Greeneville circuit	(To be supplied)	45·00
Hawkins circuit	J. Tate	40 00
Horse Creek circuit	(To be supplied)	45 00
Limestone circuit	H. Jones	40 00
Midway circuit	Wm. Mills	45 00
Mineral Hill circuit	Wm. Bluford	45 00
New River circuit	(To be supplied)	40 00
Russellville circuit	A. Gillespie	45 00
Sevierville circuit	A. Jordan	45 00
Wm. M. Haskell, Sunday-school Agent		250 00

B. H. JOHNSON, *Secretary.*

COMMITTEES OF EXAMINATION
FOR 1880 AND 1881.

ADMISSION ON TRIAL.
M. WILLIAMS,   ALEX. GILLESPIE,   H. N. BROWN.

FIRST YEAR.
A. J. FLETCHER.   A. DOUGLASS.

SECOND YEAR.
O. N. HYPSHIRE,   A. JORDAN.

THIRD YEAR.
WM. H. ROGERS,   D. B. LAWTON.

FOURTH YEAR.
WM. M. HASKELL,   WM. BLUFORD.

LOCAL DEACON'S ORDERS.
O. N. HYPSHIRE,   A. J. FLETCHER.

LOCAL ELDER'S ORDERS.
WM. H. ROGERS,   WM. M. HASKELL.

CHAT
Chattan
Marion
Chattan
Washin
Kingsto
McDona
Bradley
Knoxvi
Ebenez
Roberts
Riceville

To

MOE
Limest
Midway
Sevierv
Russell
Hawki
Minera
Coal Cr
Watau

To

GENERAL STATISTICS No. 1.

CIRCUITS AND STATIONS	MEMBERSHIP				BAPTISMS		CHURCH PROPERTY							S. SCHOOLS			BENEVOLENT COLLECTIONS												MINISTERIAL SUPPORT		
	No. of Probationers	No. of Full Members	No. of Local Preachers	No. of Deaths	No. of Children Baptized	No. of Adults Baptized	No. of Churches	Probable Value	No. of Parsonages	Probable Value	Paid on Building and Improving Churches and Parsonages	Paid on Old Indebtedness on Church Property	Present Indebtedness on Church Property	No. of Schools	No. of Officers and Teachers	No. of Scholars of All Ages	For Missions (From Churches)	For Missions (From Sunday Schools)	Total	For Woman's Foreign Missionary Society	For Board of Church Extension	For Tract Society	For Sunday School Union	For Freedmen's Aid Society	For Education	For American Bible Society	Other Collections	For Pastors, Presiding Elders and Bishops	For Conference Claimants	General Expenses, etc.
CHATTANOOGA DIST.																														
Chattanooga	36	300	5		17	1	1	8,000 00			800 00	912 00		1	13	350	350 00	94 00	640 00	15 00	15 00		15 50	700 00		90 00	91 00	914 00	84 00	200 00
Marion Circuit	4	15	1		4	1	3	350 00	1	350 00	70 00			1	8	51	1 25	50	1 75		25					30		120 00		7 00
Chattanooga Circuit	24	65	2		9	3	4	100 00			31 00			1	9	64	1 00		1 00	10		10				25		114 00		7 00
Washington	10	65	5		36	5	2	100 00			35 00			1	8	15	1 00	25		10	10			25		40		200 00		5 00
Kingston	5	50	3			7	1	700 00						1	5	28	1 50	50	2 00	25		15		50		50		240 00		35 75
McDonald	8	60			72	1		70 00			120 00		1 00	1	8	30	1 00	60	1 60	9		10	10	50		20		81 00		1 00
Dudley	19	60	2		10		1	200 00						1	13	105	1 00		1 00	10		10	5	50		30		112 00		9 45
Knoxville	5	90	5		5						2 10			1	10	122	6 50	5 00	12 50	25	1 25	3 00	1 20	50		60	4 25	300 00		4 75
Elverton	15	100	3		31		1	750 00					15 00	1	8	45	5 00	15	5 00	25	2 25	1 00	3 00	1 00				145 00		
Robertsville	9	25																												
Riceville	16	64	2		50	5	1	8 00						1	7	45	50	15	45	2	20	4		15		16		200 00	10	5 00
Total	139	1,104	27	10	54	90	12	8,250 00	1	50 00	314 15	94 00		20	100	900	40 15	10 70	66 40	65 00	25 25	5 00	11 00	20 70	4 00	2 10	10 25	2,750 50	4 45	350 00
MORRISTOWN DIST.																														
Limestone	15	150	3		8	2		1,200 00					50	2	6	110												250 00	25	
Midway	12	200	1	3	17			250 00			1 00			3	10	140	1 00	25	1 25		1 00	10		20			10	100 00	10	
Newberry	4	75			1	3		75 00						3	9	110	2 00		2 00			50						100 00	25	
Russellville	3	240	6	5	15		2	1,000 00			1 000 00		1 00	3	13	200	2 00		3 00	1 00	40	50		4 00		50		225 00	25	
Hawkins	50	100	2	3	10	6	5	780 00			780 00			3	34	180	2 00				20	30			25		50	50 00		
Mineral Hill	35	75	3	3	10		2	100 00			100 00	20		3	10	70	1 00	10			10							37 00	10	
Coal Cre.	37	75			5	10	1	80 00			80 00			2	15	130	7 0		70		50			1 00	1 00	1 00		143 00	20	
Watauga	50	300	5	1	25		2	645 00			645 00			3	20	224	1 00		1 00		60	1 00	1 00	3 00	1 00	1 00		300 00	10	
Total	100	1,391	24	34	81	225	22	5,850 00			5,850 00			35	110	1,600	0 75	90	6 95	1 00	2 90	3 00	2 00	3 25	1 00	1 75	1 90	813 00	1 80	55 00

No. of Library Books.	Total Expense of Schools this year.	No. of Sunday School Advocates taken.
00	$20 00	....
24	225 00	....
75	......	....
40	13 00	....
00	12 00	....
50	2 60	....
30	3 00	....
25	8 00	....
..	4 40	..
30	......	....
74	288 00	
..	1 50	....
50	......	....
..	10	....
1	8 00	4
50	8 00	....
50	3 00	....
8	25	....
1	20 85	4

WM. M. HASKELL.

GENERAL STATISTICS No. 2.

CIRCUITS AND STATIONS.	PROBATIONERS.						MEMBERS.						MINISTERIAL SUPPORT.			PRESIDING ELDER.		BISHOPS.		CONFERENCE CLAIMANTS.	
No. on the Roll at the Last Conference and Received Since.	No. Removed by Death.	No. Removed without Certificate.	No. Dropped, Withdrawn, or Expelled.	No. of Deaths.	No. Received into Full Connection.	No. on the Roll at the End of This Year.	No. Received by Certificate.	No. Received from Probation.	No. Received without Certificate.	No. Removed without Certificate.	No. Withdrawn, Expelled or Died.	No. of Deaths.	No. of Known Members at the End of the Year.	Pastor's Claim, including Rental Value of Parsonage, or House Rent.	Pastor's Receipts, including Rental Value of Parsonage, or House Rent.	Deficiency.	Amount Assessed.	Amount Paid.	Amount Assessed.	Amount Paid.	Amount Assessed.	Amount Paid.
CHATTANOOGA DIST.																						
Chattanooga.............	10	....	....	2	1	13	35	10	5	....	....	6	5	521	$950 00	$950 00	....	$200 00	$200 00	$4 00	$4 00	$4 00	$4 00
Marion Circuit..........	3	....	....	4	....	4	....	2	....	....	....	2	....	32	300 00	90 00	$207 00	40 00	20 00	1 00	1 00	1 00	25
Chattanooga Circuit....	2	....	3	2	7	24	....	2	....	2	....	3	....	250 00	68 00	141 00	40 00	20 63	1 00	1 00	1 00	25
Washington Circuit.....	4	....	3	al	....	5	1	4	2	3	3	6	....	85	250 00	65 00	180 00	25 00	25 00	1 00	1 00	1 00	63
Kingston Circuit........	7	....	1	1	6	14	3	3	6	29	60	1	457	302 00	124 00	145 00	35 00	25 00	1 00	1 00	1 00	35
McDonald...............	6	....	....	....	16	8	2	10	1	....	....	60	250 00	75 00	175 00	30 00	16 75				
Bradley.................	4	....	1	2	17	10	13	1	2	....	50	220 00	47 00	173 00	37 50	24 00	1 00	1 00	1 00	25
Soddy..................	17	....	....	....	21	7	2	....	....	350 00	185 00	165 00	40 00	....	1 00	1 00	50
Knoxville..............	9	....	....	2	26	7	14	....	7	98	300 00	75 50	224 50	60 00	24 71	1 00	1 25	15 00	13 85
Ebenezer...............	....	6	....	21	3	105	12	6	....	21	105	5.00 00	66 00	234 00	40 00	13 00	25	1 00
Bakersville.............	....	....	....	....	....																	
Riceville...............	1	....	....	4	16	4	4	....	5	....	41	300 00	86 55	213 45	25 00	7 44	1 00	....	1 00	....
Total........	90	6	4	37	8	129	248	49	64	22	20	107	15	1,082	3,522 00	1,576 10	1,945 00	602 50	173 38	13 50	12 23	25 00	20 05
MORRISTOWN DIST.																						
Limestone..............	15	....	....	....	13	15	....	10	....	....	....	200	200 00	40 00	100 00	20 00	10 00	....	20	....
Midway................	12	....	....	2	18	10	....	12	....	6	5	200	213 00	150 00	83 00	20 00	11 00	....	25
Sevierville.............	....	....	....	....	....	4	....	....	1	1	75	100 00	44 00	56 00	20 00	19 00	....	50
Russellville............	3	....	....	4	47	3	2	47	....	5	3	5	214	175 00	40 00	95 00	25 00	20 00	1 00	50	50
Hawkins...............	26	1	12	....	17	130	2	2	1	12	....	1	150	100 00	22 00	138 00	30 00	19 00	6 00	50	10 00	2 50
Mineral Hill...........	....	....	....	....	4	77	....	8	....	....	77		22 00	22 00		10
Coal Creek.............	18	2	....	6	13	22	1	15	2	....	4	70	202 00	130 00	132 00	25 00	14 00	....	50
Watauga...............	17	....	....	3	15	75	....	3	....	4	200	275 00	200 00	75 00	10 00	4 50	50	50	50
Total........	91	3	12	12	11	179	486	8	173	3	18	20	24	1,201	1,307 00	606 00	731 00	172 00	107 50	7 50	1 75	11 00	5 60

CIRCUITS AND STATIONS.	No. of Sunday Schools.	No. of Officers and Teachers.	No. of Scholars of all ages.	No. of Scholars 15 years old and over.	No. Scholars under 15 years old, except Infant Class.	No. of Scholars in Infant Class.	Average Attendance of Teachers and Scholars.	No. of Library Books.	Total Expense of Schools this year.	No. of Sunday School Advocates taken.
CHATTANOOGA DIST.										
Chattanooga.............	1	15	250	15	141	34	150	200	$20 00	....
Marion Circuit............	2	6	51	30	21	7	35	124	225 00	....
Chattanooga Circuit......	3	6	64	20	24	20	40	75	......	....
Washington Circuit.......	3	8	8	75	50	20	5	40	13 00	....
Kingston Circuit..........	1	7	75	10	12	18	20	100	12 00	....
McDonald.................	2	5	50	....	....	....	....	....	......	....
Bradley..................	2	13	155	50	60	45	90	250	2 60	....
Soddy...................	2	4	82	40	25	77	50	30	3 00	....
Knoxville................	2	10	122	30	62	30	108	125	8 00	....
Ebenezer	3	14	119	48	54	17	98	....	4 40	....
Robertsville	....	....	25	....	....	....	....	....	......	....
Riceville.......	2	7	45	11	25	10	35	30	......	....
Total..	23	95	1,046	329	474	278	631	974	288 00	
MORRISTOWN DIST.										
Limestone................	2	8	110	....	....	....	....	....	....	....
Midway..................	4	10	180	....	....	....	....	....	1 50	....
Sevierville..............	3	9	110	....	....	....	60	50	......	....
Russellville.............	4	15	200	....	....	....	215	....	10	....
Hawkins.................	5	24	180	111	49	20	110	1	8 00	4
Mineral Hill.............	2	10	79	35	50	14	50	50	8 00	....
Coal Creek..............	3	11	150	50	25	15	75	250	3 00	....
Watauga.................	5	25	2?0	50	125	25	40	258	25	....
Total.................	28	112	1,209	246	249	71	550	601	20 85	4

www.ingramcontent.com/pod-product-compliance
Lightning Source LLC
Chambersburg PA
CBHW031752090426
42739CB00008B/981